THE GOODS

IN YOU

How to Mark Your

Startup Ideas for Success

A Live On Your Mark Book

SpotBerry Publishing

ISBN: 0692595449

THE GOODS IN YOU

IN YOU

How to Mark Your

Startup Ideas for Success

LOWELL FORTUNE

The Man Who Thinks He Can

If you think you are beaten, you are;

If you think you dare not, you don't.

If you'd like to win, but think you can't

It's almost a cinch you won't.

If you think you'll lose, you've lost,

For out in the world we find

Success being with a fellow's will;

It's all in the state of mind.

If you think you're outclassed, you are:

You've got to think high to rise.

You've got to be sure of yourself before

You can ever win a prize.

Life's battles don't always go

To the stronger or faster man,

But sooner or later the man who wins

Is the one who thinks he can.

~ Walter D. Wintle

Look Beyond No

Lead your life to happiness. The kind of happiness you desire, fashion it with your own hands. Always remember, "NO" simply means a new opportunity for you to create, develop and become.

This book is dedicated

To my children: Kanajah, Jaalam and Kathleen, I'm ever so grateful that you, life's most precious gifts were given to me. Thank you for being my muse, my drive and beacon of hope. I challenge you to be courageous, ask questions and seek answers. In all that you do, know that you are loved, strong, smart and given to be received.

A special thank you goes out to my sisters Jeridale and Cynthia for their support and unspoken reminders of what's most important in life.

CONTENTS

THE GOODS IN YOU

Hard is easy in disguise.

~ Jaalam H. Fortune

ABOUT THE BOOK ->

Any idea that is held in the mind,

that is emphasized,

that is either feared or revered,

will begin at once to clothe itself

in the most convenient and appropriate

physical form available.

~ Napoleon Hill

The aforementioned quote doesn't put a limitation on the concept of an idea, your idea, and neither should you! It does, however, point out four essential elements for an idea to take physical form:

- An idea needs to be held (persist in the mind).

- An idea has got to be emphasized (made a priority).

- An idea must be feared (held in high regard).

- An idea requires being revered (viewed as awesome).

With, and only with, those four elements in place, your idea, without hesitation, will move to find the physical form that best provides a unique place for it on this side of reality – for all to see.

This book was written to put a useful breadcrumb like trail of information at your fingertips; helpful tidbits that those who have gone before you called upon as they foraged their ideas from the dream world and set them into reality. These breadcrumb-like markers are designed to help lead, guide, and nourish you on your way, in the hopes that you'll soon be joining their ranks.

There are 39 markers, with various activities included at each point of reflection throughout the book. As you make your way through the markers, take time to consider the questions and answer thoughtfully; just don't stay there too long. Should you discover that you come up short after completing one marker, feel free to make note of it and set a goal to achieve that marker. Setting and working toward reaching specific goals will help you **GO A**fter **L**ife **S**trategically, which requires committed action on your part.

Assuming you follow along and put forth the effort asked of you throughout this book, by the end of it you'll have exposed yourself to 39 success markers to help make your idea(s) viable, with a stronger belief in yourself, less headaches, and hopefully more resources like time, health, equity, relationships, and money than you would've had if you hadn't consciously examined and addressed these markers.

What will you learn?

As you work your way through the 39 markers, you'll learn: how to mold your idea into something people want; the secret formula to 1% mindset; what questions to ask to help you decide If you should be the one to perform the task; the 3 factors to look for when looking for a partner; the roles people, praise and you play towards success; how to nurture and build an on-line community around your idea; how to avoid underestimating people;

10 ->

9 reasons to go after smaller markets; 10 reasons to have a greater purpose than money; and how to welcome criticism while objectively looking for the hidden jewel left behind to improve you. Though extensive, this is by no means an exhaustive list of what you can expect to glean from this book.

No matter what you do in life, you have choices...

Lead or be led

Rule or be ruled

Move or be moved

Just remember that, like the fox in the hunt, it's the ruled that becomes the game.

My hope herein is that you will find this book useful in making a conscious decision to live on your mark by getting in alignment with that which you have to contribute to the world. Keep in mind that everything we use or consume is a result of someone's idea...add value to yourself and others by recognizing THE GOODS IN YOU!

Whether positive or negative, at the end of it all you will leave your mark. Leave the best you can, based on how you've lived your life to the fullest. It's time for you to rule the game.

ABOUT THE AUTHOR ->

Lowell Fortune is a web developer, graphic designer, product developer, youth developer, speaker, golf coach, and a former US Air Force Missile Combat Crew Commander with 12 years of military experience. With all that experience under his belt, the guy knows a thing or two about setting goals and having markers to live by.

Since exiting the Air Force in 2002, he's worked in sales; from high-end furniture to cars, and eventually selling health clubs to investors, each desperately searching for a way to get out of the rat race and rule their game instead of being ruled by it.

Lowell's start-up experiences include a magazine, an apparel line, and graphic design company. As a result, over the past 13 years, through research as well as personal experiences, he's come to learn how vitally important these 39 markers are to ideas, and in most cases, life.

These markers were born from studying 50 entrepreneurs heading some of the leading tech and service companies like Google, Facebook, Dropbox, Amazon, Apple, eBay, LinkedIn, Twitter, Y Combinator, Foursquare, Instagram, reddit, PayPal, Groupon, Virgin, SoundCloud, and Pinterest, just to name a few.

According to Lowell, ideas are life's most precious gems – the one true resource that will never be exhausted. Once you learn to harness their power and wield them, you can do some of the most amazing things!

It's been said that necessity is the mother of invention. Making the decision to breathe life into your idea is not only necessary, but also that which makes it possible for you to go from amazed to amazing.

Admittedly, this is Lowell's first book. Though he's been researching and studying business trends throughout the majority of his adult life, the procrastination bug bit him once upon a time. It wasn't until he made up his mind to start implementing these markers into his own life that this book came to be. Now, with a clear sense of purpose and newfound perspective of what it means to live on your mark, rest assured this won't be his last publication...

Embrace yourself and you will find true passion.

~ Jaalam H. Fortune

HUDDLE UP! ->

In the immortal words of Ralph Waldo Emerson, *The whole course of things goes to teach us faith. We need only obey. There is guidance for each of us, and by lowly listening we shall hear the right word...*

The power of your want holds the ability to lift you from small beginnings to positions of power and wealth; desire is powerful enough to snatch you from the grips of death. Desire is the voice that resonates deep within, from every fiber of your being, loudly proclaiming...

Impossible is nothing!

On your soul, nothing is impossible!

With all of our commitments and obligations, we have few commodities within our control, time topping the list of that which we hold within our grasp. Unfortunately, we so often fail to consider its value.

There isn't an abundance of time available for the taking – you only get what you get (and you don't throw a fit, right?). We're all given the same amount of time, and for each and every one of us it's our most valuable commodity; our precious nonrenewable resource. When we trade time for idle hands with running lips, we're not adding value. There is no productivity in just talking.

What a person does in his/her few "free" moments not only makes it possible to bring about a profit, but also increase mental activity. It's said that good things come to those who wait. But, more appropriately, good things come to those who act with purpose.

> *Procrastination is one of the most common*
> *and deadliest of diseases*
> *and its toll on success and happiness is heavy.*
> ~ Dr. Wayne W. Dyer

The world is forever changed by ideas, goals, and plans conceived in the minds of those who actively pursue their dreams. Likewise, habitually accepting conditions set forth by fear insures the foothold of mediocrity on your life.

So, I'll ask: how much of your talent is being wasted because you lack the boldness to put a demand on it? Creativity and success in one area of your life, in most cases, affects other areas, so start creating! The biggest difference between those who wish and those who do is motivation infused by action.

TIME KEEPS TICKING

Every second of every minute of every day, we practice and perfect the art of cowardice by trying not to rock the boat or ruffle any feathers. We further perpetuate it be choosing to believe the lie that in doing so, we are assuring ourselves security. Unfortunately, for the vast majority, the result is that we cheat ourselves and our loved ones out of what should be ours for the taking.

Dost thou love life?
Then do not squander time,
for that is the stuff life is made of.
~ Benjamin Franklin

LEARNING BEYOND OUTCOMES

If you get locked into a mindset solely based on outcomes, it will wear away at your confidence in not only your ideas, but also your effort and hard work, to the point that you'll even begin believing that, in the grand scheme of things, they don't matter. You'll start to accept that outcomes are based on luck, being in the right place at the right time, or the name on the back of your jersey. The danger therein is that your self-worth becomes contingent upon results, and like a leaf to the wind, you're enslaved. The ruled becomes the game.

Think about what it's like when you're trying to learn something. Though it seems counterintuitive, many times if you fight to stay in control, you'll slow yourself down, if you learn anything at all. For example, when you're learning to play golf, gripping the club tighter causes your arms to stiffen up. As a result, your swing will be anything but the smooth whip-like motion necessary to deliver the club face to the ball. You won't hear the coveted *SMACK!* before shielding your eyes from the sun, following the ball as it flies effortlessly down the fairway. But, that's a story for another time...

Likewise, when you let go of your need to be in control and surrender your beliefs about yourself, you allow your mind to expand and increase your ability to extend who you are.

EXPECTING THE EXPECTED

It's said that when a cruise ship went down near the Madeira Islands, there was a man among the lifeboat survivors dressed neatly in a suit, carrying a briefcase. As he climbed aboard the *rescue ship* and calmly aided other survivors, an officer congratulated him on his composure, seeking an explanation, to which the man replied:

I'm an Englishman, Sir. It is expected of me.

It was clear that this man lived in a state of expectation, and those expectations governed his actions.

In the book of *Job* (chapter 3, verse 25), he laments...

...the thing that I have feared the most

has come upon me...

That which Job focused on, though negative, was sure to seek him out. It happens to us as well. So, what if we expect what we desire the most to come upon us as a result of our expectations through faith? That seemingly simple paradigm shift would surely change everything!

Some time ago, I came across a story about a man who was observing his 100th birthday. Walking like a man nearing retirement, he proudly showed off his rose garden to a group of visitors.

To what do you attribute your long life and excellent health? they inquired.

I just never expected anything else, he responded. *I expected I'd live to see 100. I expected to be well. I expected to be just what I am, so there is no miracle about it at all.*

17 ->

Expectation is the key component necessary to generate the qualities that stick in the subconscious, formulating the new pattern of thinking you'll need to attain your goals. Those who have achieved great things thought big, visualized greatness, hoped greatly, and remained grateful during every stage of the journey.

Great expectations are your most trusted companions in life. Believe in them and anticipate that they will move with and for you in life.

Invite them to join you on your journey. In so doing, keep in mind that, unlike people, great expectations will never impose themselves upon you. They will, however, always expect you to impose yourself upon them.

THE GOODS IN YOU

Keep in mind that what you've made of your life up to this point is your very first startup. By now it should be clear that this book isn't just about ideas and startups; it's also relevant and applicable to life. The 39 markers are broken down into 5 distinct chapters, respectively titled:

- Start

- Commit

- Opportunities

- Responsibility

- Engage

SCORE!

Everything in life revolves around a score. You're scored for your growth rate from birth to age 6, you're scored on your mental prowess, your credit worthiness is a score, and the list goes on. From the moment you entered this world, you've been scored on factors over which you have little to no control, and those scores often govern how you view and value the goods in you.

If those goods were simply things, this wouldn't be so bad. However, these goods within you were gifted to you for the fulfillment and improvement of humanity. In most cases, the challenge is accessing those goods once you've realized they're there, because, for the majority of people they've been buried under the rubble of life.

Still, you want to score. We all want to score. I believe that hidden deep within each of us is the natural inclination to score, and score big.

Score big or...? Or what? What's a better option than going for it?

It all boils down to what's identifiable in your DMA: desire, mindset, and action. These are the excavators of the goods stored in you. Open your mind to the possibilities and know that some goods require that you put a demand on them. The goods in you are great, and success awaits you.

If success had a voice, I believe its proclamation would read something like this:

I will put you through hell, I will put you on your knees. I will squeeze you for every breath, every hope, and every dream.

I will take every ounce of energy you have. You want to be called by me, a success; this is what's required of thee.

19 ->

So...

Get on your mark, folks! Figure out exactly what you desire.

Get set! Get your mind fixed on committing to your desire(s), seeking out opportunities for which you'll take responsibility regarding the outcomes.

Go! Engage in persistent action through doing whatever it takes to make it happen.

ON YOUR MARK,

embrace yourself

GET SET,

your will and mind

GO!

and live your true passion

21 ->

START ->

MARKER 1 ->

PASSION

Follow your passion,
be prepared to work hard and sacrifice,
and, above all,
don't let anyone
limit your dreams.
~ Donovan Bailey

Whatever you do, make it something you're passionate about instead of mindlessly chasing the hot current trend. While you're finding and/or working on your passion, continuously strive to increase it through self-development.

When you focus your passion on all that you do, it gives you the power to become an influential pioneer. You'll blaze the trails few will have the audacity to travel down, while you'll have the will to experience their unique beauty all the way through to the end.

Your passionate pursuit of converting your ideas into reality will open doors to endless possibilities not only for you, but also those around you. Success begets success.

Expose yourself to people who are already doing what you want to do, who are the kind of people you want to be, and who love the things you love. In so doing, you'll clarify your vision of becoming that in your own way and doing whatever it is that you've chosen to do in your own time.

Point of Reflection

- What are you passionate about doing?

- Do you love it to the point that you can't see yourself doing anything else?

- If you could create your perfect day, what would it look like?

- According to your friends and family, what gets you excited?

- To what extent is your passion in alignment with what you currently do?

MARKER 2 ->

GENERATE IDEAS

Ideas can be life-changing.
Sometimes all you need to open the door
is just one more good idea.
~ Jim Rohn

Good ideas are more common than, and can help resolve, many basic challenges in our daily lives. But, while the ideas that move the scales are often unexpected flashes of brilliance and inspiration, it's the mundane thoughts hijacking the majority of our brain's time and energy that hinders our movement forward in life.

To work on developing your idea-generating prowess, you must take purposeful steps, with focused intention, in a new direction. By setting aside periods of time for observation and self-reflection, you'll be able to find and introduce new activities/behaviors into your routine.

Begin to socialize beyond your usual circle of friends, as this will open up opportunities for new perspectives (and new ideas!). Seek out those who are in a different place in life – one in which you'd like to be. For a time, you'll likely be uncomfortable, but I guarantee doing this will alter the way you think. Delve into the habits of those who are more successful than yourself, and determine to break some of your...not-so-helpful...habits. You are looking to change your life, after all.

Read more books to create new thoughts (just put aside romance novels for a time – that's not what I'm referring to here). Amazon's "Look Inside!" feature is a wonderful way to incorporate new thinking, by allowing you to get a glimpse of what a book you may not have previously purchased is all about...though, now you'll probably be all over it!

Use the web as a means to travel through the space and time of information, but remember that time is a gift given but once; use it wisely.

Purpose to generate 10 ideas daily. At first, don't put too much thought into the feasibility of the ideas; just make sure you record them. The more senses you utilize, the better, so say them aloud to yourself so you can hear them. Write them down. Type them if you want to. Just find ways to solidify them in your psyche so they have room to develop. Draw out your ideas, if you'd like, to give them structure. At this point in the game, stick figures are sexy! There's no judgment about your artistic ability – just solidify them in your mind.

As you go through your day, consider the products and tools you use, whether it be around the house or on a phone app. Where is there room for improvement? Use those *Wouldn't it be cool if we had a ...?* thoughts to change your life! Whenever you find you don't like something you're using, figure out why. From there, what would you do differently? That's your idea.

LIFE SECTOR ATTRIBUTE METHOD

According to Forbes, the richest titans of the world work in the finance, health care, insurance, retail, technology, and natural energy (oil, gas) industries. If you research common industries across the globe, you'll discover that there are 20 industries that consistently show up in developed countries. Upon closer examination, you'll find that of those 20, there are 10 sectors (or industries) most societies have in common, regardless of its level of advancement.

10 WEALTH SECTOR INDUSTRIES

1. Food

2. Transportation

3. Communication

4. Construction

5. Clothing

6. Health

7. Finance

8. Education

9. Energy

10. Technology

I believe each of us was born to address a need in one or more of these wealth sectors. How does your talent or skill set address a need in these areas?

For most of you, there's likely a disconnect here. Someone dropped the ball or failed to prepare you by not influencing your thinking along these lines. That's not cool, but now you know.

Since these sectors are common in virtually every society around the world, as you begin to think of ideas that could address these issues, you'll be sure to come up with an idea that people truly want.

LIFE ATTRIBUTES

During my time studying life as we know it, I've come to realize that there are 5 life attributes common to all, no matter ethnicity, socioeconomic status, or IQ. These common life attributes are time, health, education, relationships, and finance.

When you combine the 5 life attributes and the 10 wealth sectors to generate your ideas, you increase the probability that you will produce something, or come up with an idea, that somebody will want enough to pay for it.

Yeah, buddy!

Studies show that if you do something for 30 days you have a good chance of converting that action into a habit. So, over the next 30 days, use the Life Sector Attribute Method to generate 2 ideas for each attribute under each given wealth sector.

Below is a sample of the method using the food life sector. The goal is to think of, and list, ideas dealing with food (life sector) as it relates to the life attributes of time, health, education, relationships, and finance.

This is where your *What if we…?* and, again, *Wouldn't it be cool if we had a…?* ideas come into play. How can our fascination with food combine with the above attributes to better our society in some way?

Here's where things get fun. This is your chance to get creative… What could you create or develop?

27 ->

In regard to the **Time – Life Attribute**:

- A device that could cook a turkey in 5 minutes (less hungry family members waiting for dinner? Perfect!).

- Bake a cake in 3 minutes (no more microwaved glop in a cup!).

And food as it relates to the **Health – Life Attribute**:

- A dish that cuts your cholesterol by 25% (gotta love that!).

- A drink that removes facial wrinkles (you'll be taking advance orders in no time!).

What could you do with the **Education – Life Attribute**? How about:

- An on-line course to become a chef in 30 days.

- Blog of recipes for meals in 5 minutes or less.

When it comes to the **Relationships – Life Attribute,** what do you want to see take place?

- Restaurant where couples create a special dish together.

- Finger-foods restaurants, for couples to feed each other.

And last, but by no means least, let's look at the **Finance – Life Attribute**:

28 ->

- Delivery trucks that weigh 30% less (with decreased emissions AND less wear-and-tear on the roads).

- Food packaging that can also be used as an alternative fuel source (are you freaking kidding?!?).

Now, I'm not saying these are the specific things you should go after. I am giving you a way to help categorize things, to spark your creative impulse, to get you *en pointe*.

Who cares if your ideas seem completely too far-fetched? So what if they seem unrealistic? Forget about that. Reality isn't the starting point; your ideas are. Start the engine, roll the windows down, and let 'em ride! Use the Life Sector Attribute Method and the 10 templates provided at the end of this marker to start generating your ideas.

Food – Life Sector

- Time

- Health

- Education

- Relationships

- Finance

Transportation – Life Sector

- Time

- Health

- Education

- Relationships

- Finance

Communication – Life Sector

- Time

- Health

- Education

- Relationships

- Finance

32 ->

Construction – Life Sector

- Time

- Health

- Education

- Relationships

- Finance

Clothing – Life Sector

- Time

- Health

- Education

- Relationships

- Finance

Health – Life Sector

- Time

- Health

- Education

- Relationships

- Finance

Finance – Life Sector

- Time

- Health

- Education

- Relationships

- Finance

Education – Life Sector

- Time

- Health

- Education

- Relationships

- Finance

Energy – Life Sector

- Time

- Health

- Education

- Relationships

- Finance

Technology – Life Sector

- Time

- Health

- Education

- Relationships

- Finance

MARKER 3 ->

ASK QUESTIONS

We get wise by asking questions,
and even if these are not answered, we get wise,
for a well-packed question carries its answer on its back
as a snail carries its shell.
~ James Stephens

Ask the *Why?* questions that will drive you to figure out ways to make things better. It's through asking questions that areas of opportunity can be addressed, and then strengthened, both for yourself and for those you serve. Simon Sinek's book, Start With Why, is a great resource and great read if you'd like to delve more into the power of why.

Humble yourself to learn from those who have seen ideas through to fruition before you; just because you have the world's greatest idea doesn't mean you instinctively know how to implement it. Remember that concept formation is completely different than execution. Let others' wisdom born from failures help guide your success.

Now, unless you're an attorney, don't ask questions like one; you're seeking to increase your knowledge, not prove a point. Ask questions to which you honestly don't know the answers, as successful people are often more than willing to lend a helping hand by sharing their experiences. But in so doing, prove to be respectful of their time, being prepared with questions that can't be answered on Google.

Then, be willing to quiet yourself to listen.

Point of Reflection

- Are you asking questions against what you already presuppose to be true?

- Do people really want this, and if not, then what?

- Why would someone want to buy into this idea?

- Do you frame your questions through the *What?* , *Why?*, and *How?* stages of inquiry?

- Is the part of the project you're working on utilizing the best use of your talent, or should it be delegated?

MARKER 4 ->

KNOW THE REASON WHY

No matter how brilliantly an idea is stated,
we will not really be moved unless we have already
half thought of it ourselves.
~ Mignon McLaughlin

Diligently seek out the purpose and cause of what it is that you do or desire to do. It's here that the wheat is separated from the chaff when it comes to customer loyalty, brand longevity, and actually making a difference. Determine why it's not simply "just another product" so it won't easily come and go like the tide.

Sure, you'll bring your idea into existence to create a profit, but why does your product or service exist beyond profit shares? For most people, the reason is what drives the action. Once that's put in place, you can remind your actions why you've enlisted their help.

Take water, for example, which never forgets what it is. Regardless of it being put into a glass, pot, bowl, or pool, it remains water because it understands why it exists and what it can do, given different conditions.

Keeping that in mind, know that when you fully grasp your reason why you're doing what you're doing, you've resolved that no matter what comes against you or tries to confine your idea, it will remain on course to accomplish what it set out to do through you.

See, it's through knowing your *Why?* that you increase your confidence in yourself, which is necessary for the times when others tell you that you can't do it. There will be people in your life to help you and those assigned to hinder you; knowing your why helps you decipher between the two.

As you clarify the reason behind what you're doing, you'll gain the ability to see beyond what is and understand what could be. As a result, you will embrace your fears, succeed through failures, and bring your dreams into being.

Point of Reflection - Takeaways

- Knowing your why increases your confidence.

- Knowing your why helps you distinguish between those assigned to help and hinder you.

- Figure out and take note of what makes you unique.

MARKER 5 ->

START

We think good ideas to death,
when we should be acting them to life.
~ Brian G. Jett

Though we are all gifted with ideas, starting to actually do something about them is the hardest part of the process. Not-so-funny how that works! The challenge lies in getting the ideas down on paper, talking through them, and acting on their behalf.

Through building an idea, you create the means to attract others to it. That process should foster the growth of an idea, as well as the people involved, to set it in motion. Unfortunately, for most people, the enemy within (negative thoughts and beliefs) dampers the process, as well as the spirit.

You've probably heard that you become what you think. When you think on something long enough, it begins to shift from a thought to a desire. When that desire continues to burn within, your mind fixates on obtaining it. When you mind is set and you move into action, you're breathing life into it. So, to what are you giving life to?

Understand that the moment you start, you shift your thoughts about yourself. You must!

Point of Reflection

How do you get started?

- Re-frame the way you think about yourself. Instead of dwelling on negative assumptions about yourself (e.g., *I'm not talented enough to get this done,* or *I'm not smart enough to make this happen*), shift your perception of yourself to the kind of person that gets things done.

- Break the task into small units so you'll be able to see progress. Don't look at the task as a whole, which can be paralyzing. Break it down into tiny parts that are so trivial it would be ridiculous not to do it.

- Create a reward system for yourself. When you procrastinate, identify which of your needs you're meeting, and find alternative ways to fulfill them when your task is complete. Are you avoiding failure? Flip the script, and press forward by rewarding yourself for trying.

- Let it be known publicly. When you publicly commit your business on "Front Street," you create accountability for yourself, increasing your follow-through to avoid allowing others to see you fail, especially those who'd relish in it.

MARKER 6 ->

START WITH WHAT YOU HAVE

Ideas are the beginning points of all fortunes.

~ Napoleon Hill

It's okay to start small, as long as you start! Start with what you have in-hand at the moment, using what's at your disposal. Don't despise the small beginnings of your idea, the dream you're striving to pull into the tangible world in which you live. Remember it's the little acorn that houses all that's necessary for the mighty Oak tree to rise from the earth and tower above the ground. Both have to start somewhere, and both need time to grow.

Continually ask how you'll get what's necessary to move forward rather than dwelling on the impossibility of the situation. That alone will open the floodgates of possibilities, and when one is being realized, more are sure to follow.

Find the joy in the journey, because it's through the fun of it all that you begin to drill down into the details of how to improve your product or service, over and over again. And yes, know that it will change over time. A lot. That's okay. That's great!

Purpose, from this day forward, to look at your life and ideas, forgetting about what you can't do, and ask how you can...

Point of Reflection

- What's the idea you've told yourself you can't do? Or, what's the glitch you're finding in achieving your dream?

- What are some possible ways in which you can work around that?

- Regardless of what I have or don't have, how can I make it happen? how can I win?

MARKER 7 ->

YOU DON'T HAVE TO BE THE BEST

Having ideas is like having chessmen moving forward;

they may be beaten,

but they may start a winning game.

~ Johann Wolfgang Von Goethe

You don't have to be the best; you just have to know enough to be dangerous, which reminds me of a saying from my early military years about being small, swift, silent, and deadly (though, for the sake of business, we'll go with dangerous). When you're small, you're afforded the ability to be nimble, and you have the upper hand when you leverage that. Should you continue to take steps forward, by the time your competition looks up, you'll have gained a strong foothold on market shares. Of course, you'll need to find the right people to come alongside you to help move it along at a hurriedly slow pace – moving along, but not so fast that you're overlooking details or putting the idea or your team at unnecessary risk.

Now, though you don't have to be the best to get started, you definitely have to get started to be the best. I often wonder how many ideas lie dormant because the focus was put on being the best right out of the gate, as opposed to stepping out onto the track.

The humbling fact of the matter is that there's always going to be someone better at something than you. You've got to accept that, but don't allow that to stop you from pursuing what's on your soul to do with your life.

You don't have to look far to find people in various career fields whose drive alone pushed them past those who were more gifted. So, be the best? You can strive for that, but focus on being *your* best. When you combine your best with an unrelenting drive, there's no limit on what you can do or become.

I truly believe impossible is nothing and on your soul, nothing is impossible. So, go and get your best on!

Point of Reflection - Takeaways

- Take advantage of being small

- Find the right people

- Strive to be your best

MARKER 8 ->

WELCOME CRITICISM

In criticism I will be bold, and as sternly,
absolutely just with friend and foe.
From this purpose nothing shall turn me.
~ Edgar Allan Poe

For the most part, we're conditioned to believe that criticism is a bad thing. Whoa! Sure, it can be, but one must understand that a well-thought-out critique is invaluable and worth its weight in gold. Wisely seek out critique from as many reputable sources as possible.

Strangely, your friends will probably be happy to shower you with criticism; they know your faults well, and they also want the best for you. Though it's never easy to receive, you may find a point to improve upon. The next time you receive criticism, try the following steps to help you filter through the rubble to find the hidden jewel...

6 WAYS TO BENEFIT FROM CRITICISM

1. Whether it's offered in the form of a message or through face-to-face communication, receive criticism as a gift, thanking the individual for providing valuable feedback.

2. Try to set your defenses aside so you can discover how the criticism makes you feel. It might sting a bit, make you sad, or drive you to anger. But, once you process the message received, you can move forward from it.

3. Nearly every criticism is both objective and subjective. To grow from this, find the jewel of information in the objective piece.

4. Once you find the jewel, consider potential behavioral changes you can make to strengthen yourself in that area of your life.

5. Find a trusted confidant to be your sounding board, and ask them to help you with the next step.

6. Take what you've gleaned from the criticism and begin to implement the behavior changes you've discovered necessary within yourself.

Point of Reflection - Takeaways

- Criticism is both objective and subjective.

- A well-thought-out critique is invaluable.

- Every criticism has a hidden jewel. Some are easier to find than others.

MARKER 9 ->

TAKE ACTION

When it is obvious that the goals cannot be reached,
don't adjust the goals,
adjust the action steps.
~ Confucius

Go and do… Try something, make mistakes, learn from them, and use those miscues to your advantage. Be careful not to allow people you admire or respect to tell you something can't be done because they simply don't have the courage to make it happen. You do.

You're familiar with Sir Isaac Newton's "For every action, there is an equal and opposite reaction." The ironic thing about life is that not acting (failure to act) is, in and of itself, an action. When you choose not to act on something, rest assured that at some point, someone else will. Sometimes your ideas are only yours for a season.

You don't want to be left with thoughts of what could have been, watching someone else build their dream life based upon an idea you let rot. *I thought of it first!* doesn't matter. When you've got an idea whose time has come, breathe life into it.

Point of Reflection

- What's one idea you've contemplated?

- What are three action steps you've taken on its behalf?

- Have those steps, or actions, been consistent?

- Are those action steps in line with what you want to accomplish?

COMMIT ->

MARKER 10 ->

DIFFICULTY

Patience and perseverance have a magical effect
before which difficulties disappear
and obstacles vanish.
~ John Quincy Adams

Realistically, it's so difficult to succeed that without passion you are sure to quit. Whatever you do has to be something you can sustain over time through the love it.

Difficulty and risk become your best friends when you give birth to an idea. If you can accept this fact, you will approach the process with the focus that keeps your dreams in perspective and on track. When things don't go as planned along the way, stay dedicated to the mission at hand and do not allow failed attempts to set you back.

Working hard is an essential element to converting ideas into reality, but if that's not your commitment, the possibility of seeing anything come into being is not likely.

- In the difficult times, can you stand alone until others stand with you?

- Why should clients or customers care about what you do?

These reasons will serve to propel you when the going gets tough. It's during difficulties that you need to hold steadfast, using your *Why?* to get you through.

Discover for yourself what you're really here to do. Do you exist to provide an experience through what you do? Are you here to help people unveil their true selves to the world? Your unique value comes down to the reason you do what you do. Rely on this when challenges present themselves.

Challenge yourself through the process, so that you're not blindsided when the going gets tough.

Point of Reflection

- Why do you want to do what you're doing?

- What do you bring to the table that no one else can?

- What makes your idea unique and sets you apart?

- How will the world benefit from your time on earth?

Holding fast to those beliefs will be sure to help you weather the storms.

MARKER 11 ->

UNWAVERING BELIEF

In order to succeed,
we must first believe that we can.
~ Nikos Kazantzakis

Believing in something unseen is what manifests it into the living, seeing, world. If you wait to physically see it to believe it, then you're not the one creating it; someone else beat you to the punch. The true challenge is in believing in something enough to get people to believe in it before they see it.

You can't even take action until you believe in yourself enough to handle the outcome of your decisions. Any time you shoulder the responsibility for bringing something into existence, you become accountable for the actions you take.

Most people fail to see their ideas to fruition because the unexpected challenges become more than they think they can handle, so they no longer choose to be held accountable. They lose belief in themselves to see things through, and never experience their originally expected outcome.

Point of Reflection

- Do you believe in yourself and your abilities? If so how would you rate your belief on a scale from 1-10, with 10 being the highest rating and 1 the lowest?

- How are you going to get other people to believe in your idea?

- If you don't yet fully believe in your idea, who do you have in your life you can rely on to believe on your behalf until you grow to believe in yourself?

MARKER 12 ->

NOT JUST FOR THE MONEY

The best things in life are beyond money;
their price is agony and sweat and devotion.
~ Robert A. Heinlein

Those who look for great ideas just to make money aren't nearly as successful as those who take the time to ask themselves what they really love doing, what they know something about, and what they're interested in and excited about.

There's incredible power in knowing that what you're doing, or are about to do, will make a difference in the lives of others, and the world as a whole. That power, or lack thereof, becomes evident in the services you provide and the products you create.

A love of what you're doing doesn't guarantee success, though the lack of love for what you do invariably ensures failure; it's love that keeps you coming back when you've been kicked in the teeth and find yourself flat on your butt.

10 REASONS WHY YOU SHOULD HAVE A GREATER PURPOSE THAN MONEY

1. You tend to stick with what you're doing even when you're unhappy in the moment.

2. You look forward to greeting the following morning.

3. Ideas and innovation flow with freedom.

4. It puts your cycle of misery to rest.

5. Job resentment is dissolved.

6. You don't mind working later, longer, and harder.

7. You're willing to go the extra mile.

8. Obstacles are reduced to speed bumps.

9. You do it because you want to, not just because you can or are required to.

10. It's more enjoyable at the top because you chose to embrace the journey.

Point of Reflection - Takeaways

- There's power in knowing what you're doing will make a difference.

- The lack of love in what you're doing guarantees failure.

MARKER 13 ->

COMMITTABLE VALUES

Good ideas are not adopted automatically.
They must be driven into practice
with courageous patience.
~ Hyman Rickover

This is a tough one, but when it comes to committable values, you should strive for values that are committable to such an extent that employees can be hired/fired independently of their job performance. You've seen plenty of examples of employees getting caught doing something that sheds a negative light upon the company they represent, in such a way that it could be detrimental to the health of the business.

Irene Dunne once said: If we don't stand for something, we will fall for anything. When it comes to the values that hold your company together, you must take a stance that's unshakable.

Your core values should be the principles to which you hold true within your company; regardless of data or the market, you won't be swayed. When all hell breaks loose, the degree to which you're able to maintain your conviction around those principles is the degree to which you'll find success as a company, brand, and thriving concept that continues to stand over the long haul.

MARKER 14 ->

GO FOR EXCEPTIONAL

To create something exceptional,
your mindset must be relentlessly focused
on the smallest detail.
~ Giorgio Armani

With your ideas, strive to do something exceptional for your users, whether it's in the design, community, or connection. As a small startup, it's a big advantage, because you're agile enough to focus on the details allowing you to stand out amongst your peers.

When all is said and done, this mindset can become the core of why you're in business. While you're starting out small, remember your advantage of being swift, silent, and dangerous in your exceptional approach to meet the needs of the community you support with your idea, product, and/or services.

QUICK TIP MARKERS TO GO FOR EXCEPTIONAL->

Show Customers You're the Real Deal

- Make it clear through the quality of your product.

- Implement the idea of being the real deal into your culture and your brand.

Follow the 3 P'S Millennials Look for In a Company

1. People: social consciousness.

2. Planet: global footprint.

3. Profit: by-product of 1 and 2.

2 Qualities of Truly Investable Entrepreneurs

1. Mastery over the area of your chosen venture.

   - The competitive set.

   - The market.

   - The tech used.

2. Quiet confidence: not who shows off, but through their bearing conveys their mastery.

Seek to Have a Commanding Presence

- Be knowledgeable about the subject matter; research and do your homework.

- Articulate what you have to bring to the table based on the knowledge you've acquired.

Garner Generation Z's Loyalty

- Your budget should include YouTube. This will give you face time and a fighting chance to gain their loyalty.

- Your message should reach your specific demographic and commit to connecting with them based on their location, age and interests.

- Focus on being real and truly engaged with Gen Z. That means you may have to become more flexible in your perspective in order to create something that's truly authentic.

- Don't get pigeoned holed into Facebook Gen Z has changed the landscape of social media. If you want to capture on their loyalty, your focus should turn to the front-runners, YouTube, Instagram and SnapChat.

I believe it was Saint Ignatius who said: *One rare and exceptional deed is worth far more than a thousand commonplace ones.* So, don't just aim for exceptional; make it your standard!

- Are you ready to make exceptional your standard?

- How will you get from your current state to the standard of what's exceptional?

63 ->

MARKER 15 ->

IT HAS TO BE BIGGER THAN YOU

A hero is someone who has given his or her life
to something bigger than oneself.
~ Joseph Campbell

Whatever your idea is, you have to want it so desperately that even if you didn't receive any compensation, you'd still want to see it come to life and be successful in the world because you understand and value its necessity. When an idea or dream is bigger than you, it forces you to stretch beyond the familiar and comfortable; it will test your capabilities and require you to ask more of yourself.

The bigger the dream, the greater the fire that's lit in your heart, causing your soul to be saturated with joy every time you think about it. Your reason for living is tightly woven in your desires and dreams. When they're realized within your intent to live the life intended for you, your dreams are unstoppable.

The purpose of your dream is to draw you to it, so that you may get to know it intimately.

Does your dream feel as if it's too big for you and your capabilities?

You'll know you're in the right place and your dream is bigger than you when:

- You can't let it go.

- You would give everything for it.

- It won't fade away.

- It meets an unmet need in society.

This, my friend, is a very good place to be.

Point of Reflection - Takeaways

- The bigger the dream the bigger the fire that burns inside you.

- Your dream is intended to draw you so close to what you are suppose to be doing that you won't want to leave it alone.

MARKER 16 ->

CREATING GREAT IN DOUBT

Get a good idea and stay with it.
Dog it, and work at it until it's done right.
~ Walt Disney

When you're trying to do or create something great, if you're not feeling doubt or second-guessing whether or not it will work, you're probably not stretching or pushing yourself enough. You're not stepping out of your comfort zone.

William James said it best when he stated: *The greatest weapon against stress is our ability to choose one thought over another.* When you're creating something great, there will be doubt. The question is how long you'll allow it to occupy your thoughts.

What thoughts do you have on standby to choose in place of those doubts?

In Theodore Roosevelt's words of wisdom: Great thoughts speak only to the thoughtful mind, but great actions speak to all mankind, we find that a great thought is local in nature. It's not until the thought is given action that humanity is spoken to on a global level.

It's not just doubt that destroys greatness; it's the lack of a willing spirit to stand up to it and continue against all visible odds, through the valley, and continue to ascend the peak of one's greatness.

OPPORTUNITY ->

MARKER 17 ->

SPREADING THE IDEA

It is a lesson which all history teaches wise men,
to put trust in ideas, and not in circumstances.
~ Ralph Waldo Emerson

After the development of an idea, you need to focus on teaching and sharing your concept to get people on-board with what is to be delivered or gained through it. Keep the message focused on what's happening in regard to the industry to which your concept is appropriate. Then, build an audience willing to follow and promote your idea. The more people you have promoting the concept, especially on-line, the more real it becomes.

When translating your idea into reality, you must address these components diligently:

- Help others understand the vision.

- Clearly define your value proposition and how it can generate revenue. How much attention will it garner from investors? What moves the attention needle?

As you begin promoting your concept, it's critical to understand where and how to make your presence known. If it seems like a no brainer when it comes to social incentives and persuasive benefits, stakeholders will take a liking to the idea. The idea should swell from within a local community, live to change, and respond to changes.

While you're building a following of those who get on board with your idea, or concept, be sure your message embodies the following:

- Trustworthy – the message is consistent with the idea.

- Relevant with current trends.

- It can hold its own at being prominent – in the sea of big ideas, yours won't be squashed by others.

- Provides a vehicle allowing others to distribute the message by a means which matters most to them.

Point of Reflection - Takeaways

- Focus on teaching and spreading your idea.

- Help others understand the vision.

- The reality of the idea becomes evident when the number of people talking about increases.

MARKER 18 ->

BE MEANINGFUL

The only people in the world who can change things are those who can sell ideas.

~ Lois Wyse

Instead of focusing on how quickly you can increase the size of your idea, continue to think about whether what you've built is very important, or considerably meaningful. Then keep your thoughts on finding the best way to build out your idea, and success will follow.

Make your idea meaningful and important enough to affect the lives of others in the days ahead. Though it takes a lot of courage to let go of the familiar, what feels secure, you'll find that as you seek after what's new, you'll discover security in the unknown; it's through the gift of movement that life is brought forth, and that resultant change yields power.

Point of Reflection

- How does your idea affect the overall quality of life for other people?

- How willing are you to allow your increase to come over time, as you focus on making your idea meaning-ful?

MARKER 19 ->

SOLVE IN LAYERS

Never try to solve all the problems at once -
make them line up for you one-by-one.
~ Richard Sloma

It's great to have the expectation that your idea is going to change the world! That ambition ought to be at the core of your idea. From there, especially in the beginning stages, solving small problems in layers will allow you to build your concept in a manageable methodology, allowing you to fulfill your purpose.

How do you eat an elephant?

The answer to that question, as well as any task that can seem overwhelming, is the same.

One bite at a time!

Bite by bite, step by step, goal by goal...you attack your vision layer by layer. Ultimately, you'll unravel your concept enough to see everything as a beautifully experiential part of your journey, rather than an intimidating experience.

Point of Reflection

- How is your idea going to change the world?

- How can you implement the layered approach in your idea, and therefore, make a difference?

- What outside help, if any, is necessary to get this marker in place? Or, can your current team handle it appropriately?

MARKER 20 ->

STUDY YOUR MARKET

The purpose of human life is to serve,
and to show compassion and the will to help others.
~ Albert Schweitzer

Examine the kind of market your idea is creating, and what problem it's solving to address how you can make your concept a win-win for all involved. One exercise you may try will be to treat your day as a recipe, and account for everything you put into it to find ways to improve, become more efficient, and increase productivity. He who wields time can master the challenges of life.

In a study conducted by Bill Gross, timing (42%) was the #1 factor correlating to business success. The team, your people, came in second at 32%, followed by the idea coming in third... not too far behind...at 28%. With that in mind, know that you may start with an idea, but it quickly becomes crucial to focus the appropriate attention on its timing. Then, make sure that those you select to support the idea are on board with getting the timing right.

Did you know that Google had the initial idea similar to what we now know as Uber, but their timing was off?

Point of Reflection

- While studying the market, what have you found to be beneficial as it relates to your idea?

- Is the market hostile or friendly in regard to your idea?

- What best practices are you considering or implementing regarding the timing of your idea?

- Have you, or can you, set the right people in place to help facilitate the launch of this concept in appropriate timing?

MARKER 21 ->

SHARE YOUR IDEA

Great minds discuss ideas.
Average minds discuss events.
Small minds discuss people.
~ Eleanor Roosevelt

Share your idea! Your competitive advantage isn't centered on keeping your idea so hidden that you aren't able to discover whether or not it's truly viable. Rather, it comes from assembling the intelligence that will lead you to improve upon the idea, restructure it, or set it aside for another.

The end result is that you'll save valuable time by sharing your idea; you'll learn what the right team will look like and what turns you should or shouldn't take.

When you share your idea, you increase your pool of collective minds, helping to move it along with greater support, and perhaps at an increased pace. You alone may not be able to get the ball rolling, but someone in your trusted sphere of influence could be the catalyst.

As you share your idea and begin to act on it, you have nothing to lose. But, you have much to gain, should it lead to a positive change.

As you open yourself up to sharing your idea, you'll be amazed by how many people are willing to help you make it a reality. Give them a front row seat, as you passionately share with them that which moves you.

Point of Reflection

- In the last week, have you had a great idea pop into your head?

- What did you do about it?

- Did you at least write it down?

Uh-oh! Better write down your latest idea(s) now...

MARKER 22 ->

MAXIMIZE YOUR BEST OUTCOME

If I have a thousand ideas
and only one turns out to be good,
I am satisfied.
~ Alfred Bernhard Nobel

Maximize the probability that the person, client, or organization that knocks on the door of your idea is answered with a solved problem.

Diligently research to make sure you're not replicating something that already exists; from there, figure out what makes your concept different, trusting that you're providing something better than that which already exists. Along the way, be sure to ask the difficult questions:

- What kind of experience do I want to provide my customers?

- Why do they need (or want) what I'm trying to provide?

- How will this idea (or concept) enhance their lives?

Be open to failure as you take risks, knowing you'll gain knowledge for future success. Look for ways to get attention and stay noticed along the way. Find ways to do things differently, and seek to be impeccable in the ways you service others.

Then, be a champion of your word – deliver on what you say you'll do.

As you truly provide for your customer, you'll create a product or service that will be hard to keep on the shelves, as you'll be scrambling to fulfill service requirements. Remember that regardless of your industry, you are in the business of serving people, and that mindset will maximize your brand loyalty and sales possibilities.

Point of Reflection - Takeaways

- Due diligence is required to ensure you're not duplicating something already in the market.

- Be open to failure, for it comes with the territory.

- Do what you say you're going to do even if it cost more than you originally thought.

MARKER 23 ->

TEST ON A SMALL SCALE

You have to have an idea of what you are going to do,
but it should be a vague idea.
~ Pablo Picasso

In experience methodology, it's best to start with a small proof of concept and use it to maximize its most favorable outcome rather than going big with production before proofing the concept, even if that means running only one item through the line. Chances are, this small production will cost you more than previously planned per item, but as you bring it to reality and test its productivity, you may find flaws, as well as ways to improve upon it, thereby saving you money in the long run.

Once you have a proof of concept, get it into the hands of potential customers. Your users will be the ones best able to tell you if it's working or not; how it's meeting their needs, or even how close it is to fulfilling your original idea. From there, you can make the necessary adjustments to meet their needs, with plans of exceeding those very needs in your next version or product release.

STARTING ON A SMALL SCALE

- Begin with one.

- Maximize the most favorable outcome.

- Conduct the smallest, most cost-effective, test possible.

- Have customers use your product/service.

- Seek feedback from those who have used it.

- Make adjustments.

Your proof of concept becomes your Minimum Viable Product or MVP. MVP, a product development framework made mainstream by Steve Blank and Eric Ries which is summarized in the resource section of this book.

Point of Reflection - Takeaways

- Start small with a proof of concept.

- Get it in the hands of potential users.

- Make adjustments based on the feedback received.

MARKER 24 ->

GOBBLE THE SMALLER MARKETS

Often the difference between a successful person
and a failure
is not one has better abilities or ideas,
but the courage that one has to bet on one's ideas,
to take a calculated risk – and to act.
~ Andre Malraux

When you set out, go after small markets with the goal of taking them over before taking on the larger markets. In so doing, you'll minimize your requirements of getting started while maximizing your reach with limited resources. You'll also be able to provide a faster response to unforeseen hiccups in servicing your customer base, while protecting your new brand.

9 REASONS TO GO AFTER SMALLER MARKETS

1. Prominent positioning. Once you operate in small markets and prove yourself, the respect you gain will be worth its weight in gold as you move into larger markets.

2. Customer connectivity. You'll come to understand your customers' needs clearly, and be positioned to give appropriate solutions as they open up to you.

3. Reduced competition. Smaller markets equal fewer players. Fewer players equal more pieces of the market shares for you.

4. Investor radar. Smart investors are always on the lookout for startups that do well in niche markets.

5. Dominate the situation. When you're the "big man on campus" company, you have a greater chance of becoming the leader.

6. Innovation and freedom. You get a good glimpse into how you can improve the market, simplify the process, and reduce costs.

7. First-in bonus. By targeting smaller markets, you position yourself to garner the majority of the customer base before other players (other companies) get in the game.

8. Expansion Possibilities. Look for room to grow. Once you establish yourself as a leader, you tend to create your own space if you're looking for it.

9. Fewer Risks. Smaller markets equal smaller investments. The smaller the investment, the smaller the loss when things don't go according to plan.

Point of Reflection - Takeaways

- Set the goal to take over smaller markets.

- Service your customer base quickly and efficiently.

RESPONSIBILITY ->

MARKER 25 ->

SOUND CRAZY, JUST BE RIGHT

If at first the idea is not absurd,

then there is no hope for it.

~ Albert Einstein

It's important to note that when you unfold your big idea, your brain child, you want to sound crazy, though in the end you want to be right. According to Austin O'Malley, *A sane man often reasons from sound premises; an insane man commonly reasons as well, but the premises are unsound.*

Sounding crazy only means that you have dared to think of something, speak about it, and do something regarding it, while others were too afraid to even give consideration to it.

One of the most destructive fears is that of criticism, which has killed more ideas than any of its companions. You already know your idea sounds crazy – embrace that! Then, when criticism comes, especially from those you hold dear, it only serves to confirm the lunacy of your thought. Go ahead and sound crazy; just be prepared to defend your lunacy until sanity unveils you were right.

Dreams give each of us a sanctuary in which we can quietly and safely indulge in the insane, every day and every night of the year.

Point of Reflection - Takeaways

- Dare to think, speak and do something others are too afraid to consider.

- Embrace criticism

- It's okay that your idea sounds absurd initially.

MARKER 26 ->

DON'T UNDERESTIMATE PEOPLE

I truly believe that everything that we do
and everyone that we meet
is put in our path for a purpose.
~ Marla Gibbs

The world in which we live is filled with people who could help you; don't ever underestimate others and what they have to add to your life. Whether it's someone you see waiting at the bus stop, your server at a restaurant, your auto mechanic, or an employee of yours, they have unmeasurable worth. As you're fleshing out your idea, everyone you come across is a potential source of information readily available to you.

The smartest and most influential leaders tend to ask everyone present in a meeting what their thoughts are, because they believe everyone has worth, and want to give everyone the benefit of the doubt.

The unfortunate reality is that most of us limit ourselves to doing our best with what we're equipped with in the given moment. Learn from those around you, and lean on those who have done it before. Don't ever think you have all the answers just because it's your idea.

According to Albert Einstein, *Everybody is a genius. But if you judge a fish by its ability to climb a tree, it will live its whole life believing that it is stupid.*

Ideation is distinctly different than execution.

3 WAYS TO AVOID UNDERESTIMATING PEOPLE

1. Break out of your bubble and seek to learn about other people, especially those outside of your usual circle.

2. Know yourself and feel good about who you are, because when you're able to do that you'll be less judgmental about others.

3. When you find yourself in a conversation with someone you've just met, actively get to know them while being willing to share what you do. This approach could open doors for you as well as those you happen to meet. As always, strive for a win-win outcome.

Point of Reflection - Takeaways

- Know that people all around you every where you go are invaluable to your success.

- The smartest and most influential leaders tend to pick the brain of everyone in a given setting.

MARKER 27 ->

IT'S JUST ON YOU

There are no accidents;

we're all teachers - if we're willing to pay attention to the lessons we learn,

trust our positive instincts and not be afraid to take risks

or wait for some miracle to come knocking at our door.

~ Marla Gibbs

Though ideas should be treasured, not trampled on, know that initially nobody is going to care about your idea. It's up to you, and only you, to show the world why your idea is needed and that you're the expert to bring it forth.

Crazy though they seem, ideas should be looked at as magnificent, priceless jewels, rather than disposable napkins. The next time you come across a concept you think is a great idea, don't allow your negative self-talk to take over.

Wow – this is a great idea!

must trump

What resources do I even have to make this a reality?

Treasure and nurture your ideas. Hold them near and dear. Dust off your ideas as though you're mining for untold gold. It takes time to unveil a great idea and bring it to life for the world to see and benefit from; it's your idea for a reason – it wouldn't have been given to you if you weren't capable of giving it life.

Point of Reflection

- Now that you know that it's just on you, what are you going to do differently?

- What idea do you have that needs to be dusted off?

- You are the expert of your idea; what is your plan for sharing it with the world?

MARKER 28 ->

IS IT SOMETHING PEOPLE WANT?

Men are strong only so long
as they represent a strong idea.
They become powerless
when they oppose it.
~ Sigmund Freud

Many ideas fail because they don't fill a void of what people want. Typically, this comes as a result of producing something based on the assumption that people would want it.

In cases like that, the holder of the idea was either in denial that the product/service was needed, or someone else came along and improved upon an existing concept. Though right off the bat it's difficult to tell if your idea is something people want, you'll have a better chance of molding it while you move forward if you allow it some flexibility by implementing the Minimal Viable Product method (refer to the resources section).

Your idea should have multiple options branching off of it, like the buds on a cauliflower. If it does, you just might have a good idea. When mixed with unquenchable desire, you have a winning combination that can weather the storms of change.

Knowing the problem you want to solve, even if you don't know how to solve it at the moment, will increase your chances of generating capital and finding great people to work with you. So, finding the "pain" your potential users have will be a major factor in determining their level of want and/or need.

4 WAYS TO MOLD YOUR IDEA

INTO SOMETHING PEOPLE WANT

1. Look out for what's trending around the country; you may be able to be the first to implement something of the sort in your location.

2. Ask for unbiased opinions from people who aren't emotionally involved with the idea.

3. Get past worrying about whether or not your concept will be stolen by someone, and begin sharing it, utilizing caution and any necessary steps you can take to clear fear from your mind.

4. Consult experts face-to-face if possible. If not, research your idea's viability by employing on-line communities.

Point of Reflection - Takeaways

- Figure out early on if it's something people want.

- Your idea, like a cauliflower, should have multiple buds or options to choose from.

MARKER 29 ->

HATERS AND NAYSAYERS

You can imprison a man, but not an idea.
You can exile a man, but not an idea.
You can kill a man,
but not an idea.
~ Benazir Bhutto

Don't listen to naysayers, and do not allow other people to distract you from what you're doing. There will always be haters; they will either tell you your idea is stupid and will never work, or that you shouldn't bother working on that because someone else is more likely to produce it before you get it to market.

If you listen to negative feedback, you'll never build or prototype your idea. But, when you build things you like, chances are that there are thousands of other people who'll like what you've built and want to use them, too.

No matter what you do in life, there will be those who will judge you. Find comfort in knowing that it's just their way of casting their insecurities, negativity, and fears on you and your idea. The only critic you need to be keenly aware of is your biggest one, who has your same name and looks exactly like you in the mirror.

If not put in check, your internal critic will keep you from sharing what you're doing with friends and family; in some cases costing you the very income you're seeking, because they may know someone in need of that which you're diligently trying to provide.

Sadly, the main source of criticism comes from within. Even when it comes from elsewhere, we have the tendency to absorb, and hold onto, negative criticism longer than positive feedback, even when positivity far exceeds the negative.

So, how do you get past this?

One of the best ways is to focus on the work you're doing, moving toward fulfillment of the idea, and just let the haters hate. When you let go of what you can't control and focus on what you can, you fortify yourself against the haters and nay-sayers, because you're able to see the fruits of your labor.

Point of Reflection - Takeaways

- Listening to negative feedback in most cases leads to negative outcomes.

- Keep your internal critic in check.

- Share what you're doing with friends and family.

MARKER 30 ->

YOU CAN'T DO EVERYTHING

I know quite certainly
that I myself have no special talent;
curiosity, obsession and dogged endurance,
combined with self-criticism,
have brought me to my ideas.
~ Albert Einstein

As the founder of an idea, it's important to realize you can't do everything; even if you can, you shouldn't. Now, there are those of you who would say that you have to, and in the initial stages, that may be true. As things progress, look for people to become part of the team to help do the heavy lifting so you don't get jaded or burned out, leaving the idea to suffer and die as a result.

If you're constantly jumping from task to task, how can any one of them get your full attention? Should you find you're hopping from task to task like a grasshopper, you can use the following 5 questions to help identify what absolutely must get done.

5 QUESTIONS TO HELP DECIDE

IF YOU SHOULD BE THE ONE TO DO THE JOB

1. Am I the only person who can do this?

2. Does the idea or product benefit from me dealing with it hands-on?

3. Is this something I look forward to doing?

4. What new skill can I acquire by doing this?

5. What will have gone undone as a result of me doing this particular task?

Point of Reflection - Takeaways

- The sooner you recognize you can't do everything the better off you are.

- Multi-tasking isn't the same as doing everything.

MARKER 31 ->

FIND A PARTNER

An idea is not responsible
for the people who believe in it.
~ Don Marquis

It is imperative that you find a great partner: highly intelligent, full of positive energy, and one who possesses superb integrity. Your prospective partner needs to have all three.

Compromising on any of them could prove disastrous. For instance:

- If your partner lacks intelligence, your idea could suffer as a result of not getting the infusion of thoughts required to improve upon or guide it in the most advantageous direction.

- If your partner lacks energy he or she will buckle when it comes time to do the heavy lifting.

- If your partner lacks integrity but has intelligence along with high energy, they may sabotage the idea, running off and recreating it elsewhere, gladly sliding into the driver's seat.

After you're satisfied your prospective partner meets these requirements, you may move on to the next level of qualifications.

Point of Reflection

5 Questions To Ask Yourself About Your Potential Partner

1. Do this partner and I share the same goal?

2. Do our talents complement each other?

3. Have we previously worked together on any projects?

4. Is this partner financially stable?

5. Are there any family relations to this partner?

MARKER 32 ->

MAKE SURE YOUR GOALS LINE UP

Efforts and courage are not enough
without purpose and direction.
~ John F. Kennedy

After doing your due diligence of going through all the variables to select a prospective partner, don't overlook the importance of making sure you're both on the same page when it comes to your goals. Unfortunately, this is one of the most overlooked steps after weeding out all the obviously unsuitable candidates.

No matter how qualified a candidate appears on paper and how well they interview, if your goals don't line up you're headed for disaster. Before you launch out into the deep with someone, it's critical that you're in agreement. It doesn't matter if you want to build a small business with a few people working from home or a full-on global enterprise. You need to be on the same page.

When you initially start out, you may want to cover goals like business name, license/permit, finding a small-business advisor, and establishing a business account with a suitable line of credit.

Then you can clarify the following 3 vital goals:

- What is the purpose of the venture?

- What will the company look like in 5 years?

- What inexpensive experiments do you need to delve into while avoiding the pitfalls of the more expensive ones and still reach your ultimate goal?

Point of Reflection - Takeaways

- If your goals don't line-up success could in most cases become a pipe dream.

- Goals alignment should never be overlooked.

MARKER 33 ->

VALUES AND PRINCIPLES

A mind that is stretched to a new idea

never returns to its original dimension.

~ Oliver Wendell Holmes, Sr.

Many corporations have core values or guiding principles upon which they're founded. The problem is that they're usually lofty sounding, but lacking stickability; often forgotten within an employee's first few days.

Everyone with the hopes of making an idea successful must value relationships. Within those relationships, strive to hire talented people, treat them with respect, and qualify that they are, indeed, a good fit for your organization.

Your talented core group should be allowed to cultivate an environment of teamwork that encourages debate, so that they may develop the best possible approach to the product/service, as well as the process.

To keep a team healthy and motivated, leaders have to understand the importance of being true champions of their word. Simply put, managers can't expect to keep the team's trust if they say one thing yet do another.

As you and your team move from success to success, it's crucial that the pursuit of finding better ways to meet customer needs remains the focal point. As that's front and center, address how you'll expand product offerings and diversify skill sets, making it difficult for the competition to replicate not only your product, but also your team.

Remember that the community is where your customers live and work. Whether directly or indirectly, your mission, should you choose to accept it, is to make every effort to take the improvement of the community's quality of life into consideration.

Point of Reflection - Takeaways

- Leaders have to understand the importance of being true champions of their word.

- Finding better ways to meet customer needs must remain the focal point.

- Successful ideas are founded on valued relationships.

ENGAGE ->

MARKER 34 ->

THE IMPORTANCE OF YOUR STORY

Human history is,

in essence,

a history of ideas.

~ H.G. Wells

Recognize the importance of your story and recall it often. Your story is one of your foundational truths, both to you and your idea. Cultivate, embrace, and share it. Without this account of your progress, you may find it difficult to recover from the minutia of details regarding your product, especially during times of trial. Always consider how far you've come.

While it's vital to your progress, telling your story isn't an end; it's a way to keep yourself afloat through storms. Stories are told to teach, transcend, and transform; use yours to inspire someone, as a means of making a difference in our world.

What often goes unrecognized is that stories are gifts for future generations. To live more of your spiritual and earthly potential is the honorable thing to do.

Maya Angelou captured the power and impact of a story when she said: There is no greater agony than bearing an untold story inside you.

6 THINGS TO CONSIDER ABOUT YOUR STORY

1. Take the time to understand and develop your story so it's relatable.

2. Share your story to all who are willing to listen.

3. Seek to find the little things in your story that make it (and you!) unique.

4. Remind yourself that your story is but a small part of the collective book of humanity.

5. Your story is meant to affect you as well as others, for the good of all.

6. Your story is a gift that should be offered as often as possible.

Point of Reflection - Takeaways

- Your story is important, so recall it often.

- Stories are gifts to future generations and reminders that your current situation, regardless of it's nature, is necessary and a valuable part of your story.

MARKER 35 ->

UTILIZE ONLINE COMMUNITIES

Good ideas are common –
what's uncommon are people who'll work hard enough
to bring them about.
~ Ashleigh Brilliant

If you're not connecting through on-line communities, you're at a huge disadvantage to those who are. Use the web for feedback on your ideas, as well as suggestions about how to improve upon them.

Through on-line communities, you'll be able to form relationships with others who are passionate about your ideas; people from all over the world will come to the table with their own unique experiences and perspectives, which could prove invaluable.

By introducing yourself and your concepts in a way that allows others to be a part of the process, you can allow the internet to gain you worldwide awareness in a short period of time. What it all boils down to is that if you have something worth sharing, people will share it.

In general, nobody cares about your idea initially. Sorry to be the bearer of bad news, folks. That said, when you share an idea that touches something others care about and solves a problem they're experiencing, you'll get attention.

HOW DO YOU BUILD AN ONLINE COMMUNITY?

- Pinpoint the idea or message you want to spread.

- Provide consistent content - Know that consistency can very from once a week to every day and even multiple times a day depending on the platform. Regardless of the schedule you decide to go with it's important that you stay true to that schedule.

- Make the content sharable - Size indeed does matter. According to the top 10 percent most shared articles, you should shoot for 3, 000 to 10,000 words to make it shareable. The key is finding what works best for your community. You may find that short, quick reads work best for your followers.

- Stay involved on social media - have a really good profile on multiple networks. Connect with everyone you meet in person on social media. Listen and learn what's important to current and future clients. Post often with 1/5 of the posts going towards the organization, 3/5 going to advice and topics clients care about. The remaining 1/5 should be spent on current news and events.

- Show that you care about building community - get the executives involved on-line. Make time for engaging your on-line community.

- Empower others to spread your idea - encourage followers and non-followers to spread the idea through blogs, email and or social media. Try to figure out the why behind life, trends and the successful. Unveil how the idea will change the world. The idea should be bold, stated positively and strongly. It should be given in small quantities and built upon through short bursts. Don't let the importance of the idea drive it off the cliff of boredom.

- Promote others by helping them grow - develop real relationships with your connections followed by promoting their social content. Promote others long before you go knocking on their door for a cup of sugar. There's plenty to go around, so don't shy away from helping those in your industry or those with similar businesses. Be consistent in your promoting of others. Make promoting others a conscious and active efforts and you're sure to see the fruits of your labor both directly and indirectly.

First things first, figure out who your supporters are and what you believe they'll rally around.

3 WAYS TO NURTURE YOUR COMMUNITY

1. Once you have your audience engaged, ask them to get more involved through donations or surveys.

2. Create opportunities for them to interact and work with each other.

3. Treat your community with respect by maintaining your integrity and transparency with them.

MARKER 36 ->

TEST IN REAL WORLD SITUATIONS

An invasion of armies can be resisted,
but not an idea whose time has come.
~ Victor Hugo

Rigorously testing your ideas in real world situations throughout your product development process isn't about double-checking your vision; it's what allows you, early on, to make whatever necessary tweaks are desired before a glitch or flaw becomes disastrous in wasting time, money, and other resources that could slow production or produce a product far less in quality than you'd envisioned.

When you test in the real world, you're able to get a better sense of timing for the idea, since you're shooting for an idea whose "time has come." If you can get the timing right, you'll leave your competition in the dust.

4 WAYS TO TEST REAL WORLD OUTCOMES

1. Provide mock-ups on a store shelf and seek feedback.

2. Limited audience A/B testing (same product, different location).

3. Open a location in a small market.

4. Get prototypes into the hands of users for evaluation.

6 THINGS TO DO FOR REAL WORLD SURVIVAL

1. Review your idea with a fine-toothed comb, looking for weaknesses and how they could affect the idea.

2. Consider how, as is, your project will hold up over the course of the next five years.

3. Check your idea for sustainability against possible competitors, knowing they will come.

4. Examine scalability and flexibility of the idea to discover various ways it could be shaped to adapt and grow.

5. Discover your brand loyalty – what will keep your client or customer base loyal to you?

6. Test the idea in a real world situation, being sure to do it prior to the full-blown launch into the marketplace.

Point of Reflection - Takeaways

- Real world testing gives you the feedback you need to make the necessary tweaks that improves the product.

- Testing in the real world helps you to better assess the timing of the idea.

MARKER 37 ->

THE LUCK FACTOR

The only good luck many great men ever had
was being born with the ability and determination
to overcome bad luck.
~ Channing Pollock

Seneca said: *Luck is what happens when preparation meets opportunity*. While many people will recognize your hard work's success as "luck," it remains important to realize that taking things to the next level, beyond what you could've possibly imagined, will, to some degree, rest on luck.

The most important aspect of anything you aspire to do on a grand scale is examining its scalability. Consider how able it will be to adapt to various or increased demands. Addressing the scalability of the idea is the preparation component of luck that positions you for the opportunity. Without scalability, you've already set a build-in expiration date.

Picture whether or not this product/service is something every company will want, as well as every consumer will want to have or use. It's there that you can gage its maximum potential and set yourself up for success, even if its life expectancy is shorter than you would have hoped.

- What will it take to help you prepare for the opportunity around the corner?

- What does scalability look like for your idea?

- Is the byproduct of your idea something that every company or consumer will truly want?

Point of Reflection - Takeaways

- Scalability is the cog in the wheel of longevity.
- Can you picture the product as something everyone could use or benefit from?

MARKER 38 ->

PEOPLE, PRAISE, AND YOU

Never underestimate the power of dreams
and the influence of the human spirit.
The potential for greatness
lives within each of us.
~ Wilma Rudolph

Over time, your idea will create a company, and that company will be composed of a group of people. As the leader of the group, you have to be inspiring, a great listener, motivating, and willing to look for, in order to draw out, the best in people. And, you must be good at consistently communicating praise.

PRAISE PEOPLE

Johann Wolfgang Von Goethe eloquently stated that if you *treat people as if they were what they ought to be you help them to become what they are capable of being.*

As flowers flourish with watering, so do your team members upon receiving praise. As the leader of an idea, learning to provide praise for your team members is a critical attribute that must not be overlooked or taken for granted.

BE AN ASSISTANT

As counterintuitive as it's become in today's society, lead by assisting and supporting those you've assembled on your team. Make sure they have what they need in order to become successful in their area of expertise.

Have an open communication policy so that people may freely come to you for support, and understand that if your team is communicating their needs and they still don't have what they need to do well with moving their part of the project forward, you're the one who needs to step up your game.

Point of Reflection - Takeaways

- Your idea creates the blueprint for the company, but your people will be the ones to build it out to the specifications of the blueprint.

- The healthiness of the company begins and ends with the people and how happy they are.

MARKER 39 ->

FLEXIBILITY AND FAILURES

All the art of living lies in a fine mingling
of letting go and holding on.
~ Havelock Ellis

LET GO OF THE UNCONTROLLABLE

As you bring your idea to market, there will be many factors outside your control which could ultimately determine your success, such as proper timing, economic stability, and proper connections. Meeting the right people to help finance your idea, your company, can be one of the most critical uncontrollable factors. Keep pressing forward, expanding your circle of influence, and sharing your story.

FLEXIBILITY IS POWERFUL

Within your concept, leave room to be flexible and open-minded. Not to say that you shouldn't have a vision of what you want your idea to turn into, but great structures that withstand the test of time are able to do so because they were built with the understanding that changes in seasons will (not might!) cause changes in the materials used in construction; there's both room to flex and the ability to absorb, while maintaining the ability to withstand the elements. Keep that same concept in mind while you're creating your concept, best positioning yourself for whatever lies ahead.

EMBRACE YOUR MISTAKES AND LEARN

One of the most popular questions arising with any new idea is: *What if we make mistakes?* I'll answer the million-dollar question for you, but first you must sit down. Ok, are you ready? Here it is: *That's great!*

Make as many mistakes as you can, while being as sensible as possible. You can't possibly move forward while trying to avoid mistakes because that ensures you'll make tons of them...and when you do, they'll surely cost you. The most important thing about making mistakes is learning quickly from them so you can figure out how to capitalize off of them.

More often than not, the biggest mistake you can make is giving up. The close second? Calling it a quits just a moment too soon. It's not for you to decide when your breakthrough will come; what you can control is the extent to which you pursue it.

COURAGE AND GENIUS

There are two things that will always prove instrumental in the success of your idea. You guessed them: courage and genius. Courage is where you find your determination to keep stepping forward in the face of adversity. Though it may prove difficult, courage can be a learned skill. Genius, however, is a little tougher to pull off if you don't already have it; that's why you surround yourself by those who do. If you've got courage without genius, you've still got a shot. Genius without courage? Yeah. That's when *Good luck!* is most apropos.

GO IN WITH EYES WIDE OPEN

Go into your idea understanding that it will take hard work – lots of it, and there will be plenty of time spent doing things you don't want to do. You'll answer customer support questions or take sales calls. You might arrive early to the office to make coffee, stay late to clean the bathroom, and design a Power-point at home during your friend's envied Christmas vacation. Nothing is beneath you when it comes to achieving your goal of getting it done.

OPTIMISM HAS ITS PLACE

Look at the sunny side of what you'll learn throughout the process, defining all worst-case scenarios in terms of time loss and financial loss. From there, you'll be more accepting from the start. If you don't prepare yourself with an optimistic approach, the first time you run into a roadblock or hiccup you are too likely to throw in the towel.

THE SECRET FORMULA OF THE 1%
Problem of Possibilities (POP)

A few years ago I discovered an outlook or view point on life that I termed the Problem of Possibilities or POP. This perspective or viewpoint greatly effected how I approached life's situations. It allowed me to challenge and question the norm. As a result, I was able to see beyond the vale and peer into what I believe is the mindset of the 1%, the top income earners.

From behind this vale appeared a simple, yet very powerful math problem. Over the years I've asked people from all walks of life what is 2 + 2? I was given some of the most amazing looks and some even looked as if to say I was insulting their intelligence. But invariably they would answer 4. No surprise there! I immediately followed with the question, what if I were to ask you what is 4?

The myriad looks I received ranged from righteous indignation to are you kidding me. You could tell right away from the answers, those with a healthy grasp of numerical gymnastics and those who, well let's just say had a inclination in areas other than math and science.

As you can guess there were more than one possibility. You could see as the old saying goes, the light turn on as they blurted out 3 + 1, 8/2, 2*2, 10 - 6... At that very moment, they found themselves in tuned to the limitless power of POP (Problem of Possibilities).

When you think in terms of what is 2 + 2, you arrive at the answer of 4, unfortunately, the problem of possibilities ends there. But, when you begin to think from the perspective of what is 4, your answer like your possibilities become infinite.

So, what if you were to think like the top 1% and approach life from the perspective of what is 4 as oppose to what's 2 + 2?

What limits could be removed from your life? What possibility could you realize?

That dream could become your every day reality. That untapped idea, fueled by your passion, could be the next thing that moves us forward as a species.

Now is the time, your the time!

It's your turn to find and deliver

THE GOODS IN YOU.

RESOURCES ->

IDEA-TO-PRODUCT CHECKLIST ->

10 STEPS TO CONVERTING YOUR IDEA INTO A PRODUCT

1. Idea
   a. *How can I do this better?*
   b. Create a product design.
2. Market assessment
   a. *Who will buy my product?*
   b. Quantify your market.
3. Prototype
   a. Proof of concept.
   b. Make the prototype.
4. Refine the product
   a. Get ready for market.
   b. Test and refine.

5. Organize and make it official

    a. Think like a CEO.

    b. Prepare a business plan and purchase business cards.

6. Critical paperwork

    a. Legal documents and marketing materials.

    b. Drawings, brochures, and patents.

7. Begin production

    a. Slow and steady wins the race.

    b. Start mass production.

8. Market and sell

    a. Sell to target market.

    b. Find market niche; prepare a sales plan.

9. Find Distributors

    a. The power of volume.

    b. Find the biggest and best.

10. Manage

    a. Plan, control, manage, and lead.

    b. Develop growth strategies.

MINIMUM VIABLE PRODUCT (MVP) ->

The minimum viable product (MVP) is the product with the highest return on investment with the lowest risk. Coined and defined by Frank Robinson and made mainstream by Steve Blank and Eric Ries, MVP serves as a powerful framework for formulating market analysis beforehand.

DESCRIPTION

A minimum viable product has just the core features allowing the product to be deployed to a subset of possible customers, such as early adopters or trend-setters, who are thought to be able to grasp a product vision from an early prototype, forgiving in flaws, and willing to provide feedback.

MVP strategy aims to:

- Avoid building products that customers don't want.

- Seek to maximize the information learned about the customer, per dollar spent.

- Make and sell a product to customers.

A process of idea generation, prototyping, presentation, data collection, analysis, and learning, the primary goal is to minimize the total time spent on iteration until a desirable product/market fit is reached, or until a product or service is found to be nonviable.

MVP PURPOSES

- Be able to test a product hypothesis with minimal resources.

- Accelerate learning.

- Reduce wasted engineering hours.

- Get the product to early customers as soon as possible.

- Provide a base for other products.

TESTING YOUR MVP

- Results from MVP tests aim to indicate whether or not a product/service should be designed.

- Evaluate if the initial problem or goal has been solved in a manner making moving forward acceptable.

FOR PRODUCTS

A MVP strategy for a web application, for example, would be to create a mock website for the product and purchase on-line advertising to direct traffic to the site. The mock site may consist of a marketing landing page with a link for more information or to make a purchase.

While links are not connected to a purchasing system, clicks are recorded to measure customer interest. Real life examples can be found on-line on a daily basis.

FOR SERVICES

Commonly used for services attempting to charge customers for manually performing a service, without any specific product development. Consider an on-line radio service, playing customer-selected music based upon individual preference. You could test willingness to pay for personalization.

FOR FEATURES

Let's say you provide a link to a new feature, based upon a web application on a preexisting site. Again, the feature itself is not fully implemented; rather, an apology, mock-up, or marketing page is provided. Clicks on the link are recorded, providing an indication of the demand for the feature in the customer base.

ONLINE REFERENCES ->

MARKET WISE TOOLS

- Unomy - http://unomy.com

- Compete - http://compete.com

- Alexa - http://alexa.com

- Hoover's - http://hoovers.com

- Google - http://google.com/alerts

- InsideView - http://insideview.com

- SimilarWeb - http://similarweb.com

- Rivalfox - http://rivalfox.com

- SalesLoft - http://salesloft.com

- Lead411 - http://lead411.com

SEARCH ENGINE OPTIMIZATION (SEO) TOOLS

- Moz - http://moz.com

- Raven - http://raventools.com

- Positionly -http://positionly.com

- WebCEO - http://webseo.com

- SEMrush - http://semrush.com

- SpyFu - http://spyfu.com

- Ahrefs - http://ahrefs.com

A/B TESTING; OPTIMIZATION TOOLS

- Unbounce - http://unbounce.com

- Optimizely - http://optimizely.com

- Instapage - http://instapage.com

- PageWiz - http://pagewiz.com

INVESTOR RELATIONS/FUNDING HELPERS

- AngelList - https://angel.co

- pitchXO - https://pitchxo.com

THE GOODS
IN YOU

How to Mark Your
Startup Ideas for Success

A Live On Your Mark Book

ISBN: 0692595449

SpotBerry Publishing
3500 Vicksburg Lane N.
Plymouth, MN 55447